DEDICATED TO ALL WHO LOVE AND CARE FOR THE TREES OF PLYMOUTH

IN ASSOCIATION WITH

International Tree Foundation

Moor Trees

BTCV

City of **Plymouth**

THE Herald
THE VOICE OF PLYMOUTH

The Tree Council's Tree Warden Scheme

THE TREE COUNCIL — in partnership with National Grid and supported by the Government's Cleaner, Safer, Greener initiative

ACKNOWLEDGEMENTS

Plymouth's Favourite Trees project was set up and steered by the leading organisations of Plymouth Tree Partnership in association with The Herald and their logos appear opposite in appreciation of their commitment. The project was made possible by donations from DML Devonport and Plymouth & South West Co-operative Society, and a grant from Awards for All.

Plymouth's Favourite Trees were nominated by the people of Plymouth. The final thirty trees were selected by:

Jon Stokes, Director of Rural Programmes, The Tree Council
Esmond Harris, past Director of the Royal Forestry Society
Mel Holt, BTCV Community Tree Officer
Jackie Perry, local Tree Warden
Andrew Young, Chairman of the Plymouth Tree Partnership
Paul Padfield, BTCV Devon Manager

and from Plymouth City Council:
Nick Jones, Principal Parks Services Manager
Nick Maker, Parks Services Operations Manager
Chris Knapman, Tree Officer

**SPECIAL THANKS TO EVERYONE
WHO PLAYED A PART IN IDENTIFYING,
NOMINATING AND PHOTOGRAPHING
PLYMOUTH'S FAVOURITE TREES
AND TO THE OWNERS WHO HAVE
WILLINGLY CO-OPERATED
WITH US AND TAKEN PRIDE
IN THEIR TREES.**

CREDITS

FIRST PUBLISHED IN GREAT BRITAIN IN 2008 BY
Plymouth Tree Partnership   www.plymouthtrees.org
89 Houndiscombe Road, Plymouth, PL4 6HB

RIGHTS

ISBN   978-0-9558656-0-2

COMPILED BY
Gloria Dixon, local Tree Warden
Chris Knapman, Tree Officer at Plymouth City Council
Andrew Young, Chairman of the Plymouth Tree Partnership

PHOTOGRAPHY BY
Lucy Duval and Archie Miles

DESIGNED BY
Jo Lucas

PROJECT MANAGED BY
Dean Price

PRINTED BY
Colour Works (Print & Design) Ltd

COVER PHOTOGRAPH
Holm Oak at Nazareth House by Lucy Duval

PAPER
Cyclus paper used in the production of this book is made from 100% de-inked recycled paper and has earned the environmental status of Nordic Swan, Blue Angel and the EU Flower. The paper is acid free, chlorine free, recyclable and bio-degradable.

CONTENTS

FOREWORD

Trees are a vital part of Plymouth's regeneration effort. Without their presence in our gardens, streets and parks, all our lives would be immeasurably poorer. They provide oxygen, absorb pollution and noise, give shade and shelter from the elements and reduce stress. In short, trees are essential for healthy living.

Trees are also central to good urban design as they soften the hard edges of buildings, frame attractive views and draw perspectives. But their importance goes even wider. They create landmarks for local communities, generate countless memories and lead to a sense of identity and belonging.

It is good to reflect that trees all around Plymouth only exist because local people cared enough to plant them. In that sense, they are different from trees in the countryside which can grow naturally from seed.

Plymouth Tree Partnership exists to bring together organisations, groups and individuals who want to improve the quality of life in Plymouth by understanding and communicating the importance of trees.

This book supports that aim by celebrating some of Plymouth's best-loved trees. Many were planted by previous generations and, surviving all kinds of hazards, have grown to be full of beauty. They encourage us now to pass on that love by planting and protecting Plymouth's favourite trees of the future.

ANDREW YOUNG
CHAIRMAN
PLYMOUTH TREE PARTNERSHIP

INTRODUCTION

Great Britain has an outstanding tree heritage and Plymouth is no exception. Indeed it is one of the few cities to have a tree species named after it, the Plymouth pear. The Herald asked its readers to nominate their favourite trees and the thirty chosen for this book all tell the stories of local people.

The trees are found across the City of Plymouth and form an interesting collection linking the present with the past, showing that the importance of trees goes well beyond their natural lives. They include everything from introduced and native trees to unusual forms and gnarled veterans.

Our national tree, the oak, is well represented and particularly relevant to Plymouth as it provided the inspiration for the design of Smeaton's Tower. Plymouth is famous for its ship building and over the centuries many explorers and plant hunters have sailed from here in ships made of oak.

We should not forget that despite their strength and longevity, trees can also be vulnerable. Two prominent trees, the North Prospect horse chestnut and Eggbuckland elm, have fallen victim to decay and bad weather during the writing of this book. The memories here should help to ensure that replacements are planted and nurtured until they can take their place in the landscape once again.

There must be many other Plymouth tree stories waiting to be told. If you have a favourite tree and would like to share it with others, send your story to the Plymouth Tree Partnership or The Herald so that it might be included in a future book.

As Plymouth embarks on a new and exciting chapter in its history, with aspirations to become a major European city set against the challenge of climate change, it is hoped that these accounts will highlight the importance of trees in that future.

BLUE ATLAS CEDAR

Cedrus atlantica f. glauca

Location

The tree can be found next to Derriford Hospital, near the steps leading from upper car park A to the main hospital entrance.

Story

"The most beautiful tree to me is a cedar. This one grows right opposite the main entrance of Derriford Hospital."

"When I was a girl in 1949 I would ride ponies under it. At that time there was no hospital, just green fields. On bright mornings it looked like frost on the branches any time of the year. It was in the grounds of Derriford House, you can still see part of the wall now."

"I do not know the tree's age. I was so thankful it was saved. Each time I am there I look at it. It helps pass the time of a not so good, so called modern age."

Mrs Mary French

Did you know...

• The Atlas cedar comes from the Atlas Mountains of Algeria and Morocco. Seeds were brought here in 1839 and some of the original plantings still survive.

• The ornamental trees cultivated in British gardens have a more noticeable blue tinge than those grown in the wild. It has aromatic wood which is insect repellent.

• Unusually, the Atlas cedar flowers in the autumn, leaving a carpet of slug shaped catkins on the forest floor.

HORSE CHESTNUT
Aesculus hippocastanum

Location

Unfortunately this veteran tree had to be felled in 2007 after it had become colonised by fungus. It used to stand at the junction of North Prospect Road and Segrave Road.

Story

"It is an amazing tree standing like a lone ageing guard in a sea of tarmac and concrete. Its size, shape and energy bring natural power into the city."

Mr Clive Martin

"This wonderful horse chestnut tree stands majestically amid all the daily traffic. Just beautiful."

Mrs Jackie Ruffin

"I have been admiring it for well over 30 years now and it never fails in its beauty whatever the season. I can only guess at its age but feel it must be very, very old."

Mrs P.F Light

Did you know...

• When planted this tree stood in the grounds of Swilly House, the home of Captain Furneaux, the circumnavigator.

• The horse chestnut tree comes from Greece and Albania. It was introduced to Britain in 1616.

• Bees can tell instantly whether the flowers have been pollinated as the insides change from yellow to red.

• The wood, which is very light in weight, was once used for making artificial limbs. Interestingly, if you pull off a leaf, the scar left behind looks like a horseshoe.

THE WIDEY OAK
Quercus robur

Location

Turning into Widey Wood in Crownhill from the Widey Lane entrance, this amazing tree is standing about 10 metres down the main path.

Story

"The area gives us pleasure throughout the year. It is steeped in history and dates back to a mention in the Domesday Book. The manor house was a fine building; Royalist troops were billeted there during the Civil War and it is said that King Charles I reviewed them standing under this tree. I'm sure it could tell you many a tale if only it could talk."

Mrs Inga Gurney

"The huge bole is like a gigantic beer barrel."

Mrs Sarah Marsland

Did you know...

• The tree's trunk measures 7.2 metres (over 23 feet) all around. Its unusual shape is probably a result of pollarding over many years. Pollarded trees generally live longer than those left to grow naturally and the Widey Oak is estimated to be at least 500 years old.

• Oak was used extensively for house-building - the Elizabethan House near St Andrew's Church is a local example. It is also used for wine casks and producing charcoal.

• It is said that oak trees grow for 300 years, rest for another 300 years and then die back over the next 300 years of their lives.

CORSICAN PINE
Pinus nigra var. maritima

Location

This tree can be found by entering Ford Park Cemetery at the Ford Park Road entrance. Beyond the chapels it stands in the middle of the cemetery.

Story

"It looks like a giant umbrella which shelters me from life's storms and it shields my family's grave."

Mrs Jill Dolan

Did you know...

• Corsican pines were introduced from Corsica in 1759.

• Ford Park Cemetery was established in 1858 when the city's churchyards became full. It was the main burial ground for the three towns of Plymouth, Devonport and Stonehouse. One of the famous people buried there is John Rendle, a nurseryman and seedsman, who founded Plymouth's Royal Botanic Gardens in 1850 and planted it with trees from around the world.

• Trees have always been important in Ford Park Cemetery; the first ones were planted in the year that it opened and there is an ongoing programme of care and new planting.

• Corsican pine is a variety of black pine. Other varieties can be seen in different parts of Europe and include the Crimean pine and the Austrian pine. All are deep rooted and drought tolerant which may help them to adapt to climate change.

• Corsican pine can grow near the coast because it is able to withstand salt winds.

MONKEY PUZZLE

Araucaria araucana

Location

Access this tree by the Ford Park Road entrance to the cemetery. It can be found at the top end towards Mutley Plain.

Story

"The tree's domed crown fills this corner of the cemetery and reflects the Victorian age."

Mr Phil Armson

"It makes me smile, as it is amusing to see a female doing so well in flowering without a male nearby!"

Mrs Jill Dolan

Did you know...

• This tree, introduced to Britain in 1795, became a status symbol in Victorian times. It was discovered by a naval surgeon, Archibald Menzies, who attended a dinner in Chile and was served a bowl of its nuts for dessert. They are delicious when cooked.

• The fossilized wood can be made into jet jewellery.

• In Britain the tree is fast growing but does not live for more than 100 – 200 years. In its natural habitat, on volcanic slopes and hilly areas in Chile and Argentina, it grows slowly and lives for much longer, even 1000 – 2000 years. Its bark can be as much as 18 centimetres (7 inches) thick and resembles a tough hide.

• The monkey puzzle tree is under threat from too much logging and, while common in British gardens, it is becoming an endangered species in the wild.

HOLM OAK
Quercus ilex

Location

At the rear of Nazareth House in Durnford Street, this tree can be seen by taking the coastal path from Devil's Point towards Millbay.

Story

"Many orphaned children have played beneath it. The public out walking near Devil's Point along the front, admire it. It is one of the last big trees in England that many sailors and marines see as they sail off for foreign ports."

Mr Basil Downing-Waite

"My grandson and I get so much pleasure visiting Devil's Point, especially in autumn when we collect the acorns, still held within their silky, hairy cups from the many holm oaks growing so crookedly along the seashore."

Mrs Gloria Dixon

Did you know...

• The acorns from the holm oak tree were used as packing material for shipping Italian statues and other valuable items. When thrown out after the valuables had been unpacked, they often seeded and became plantations on estates.

• The tree grows right on the coast and many can be seen all around Plymouth Sound. Native to the Mediterranean lands, it was brought to Britain around 1500.

• It is also known as holly oak, because of the shape of its leaves. As a young plant its leaves are spiky. Both ilex and holm mean holly.

COPPER BEECH
Fagus sylvatica f. purpurea

Location

This tree stands in all its glory in Stoke village. It is situated at the top of Ford Hill at the corner of Devonport Road and Packington Street.

Story

"This tree is probably the last remaining vestige of the Old Stoke House, used as a children's home until destroyed by enemy bombing in 1944. With its roots firmly embedded in the rocky ground, it has withstood storm and tempest and is a delight to the eye. Skeletal in winter and beautifully coppery in summer, it dominates the view at the top of the hill."

Mr and Mrs Robert and Jean Yates

Did you know...

• The common beech tree produces only 1 in about a 1000 seedlings which grow coppery coloured leaves. The purple green hues of the leaves of the tree at Ford Hill pick out the colours of the slate wall beneath.

• Mature beech woods create thick overhead canopies in the summer; ideal for bluebells to flower in the spring.

• Beech wood is fine-grained and makes good furniture. It can be steamed and bent into curved pieces like the rockers for rocking chairs. It is also good for parquet flooring and a popular timber for wood turning.

• Beech leaves collected before the first frosts were used to stuff mattresses and were said to last for six or seven years.

PACKINGTON STREET
Nos 53 - 70

29

SMOOTH LEAVED ELM
Ulmus carpinifolia

Location

No longer there to be admired, it was to be found halfway along Charfield Drive in Eggbuckland.

Story

"This is a survivor, having lived through three outbreaks of elm disease (in 1920s, 1940s and 1970s)."

Mr Phil Armson

"This tree was planted when Eggbuckland was just farmland in a country hedge. Two crows always nest in it every year and rear two or three chicks. I love this tree, its beautiful shape and although open to all the bad weather, it's so tall and has held its ground."

Mrs Margaret Turner

Did you know...

• Having survived Dutch elm disease for so many years, it was particularly sad that abnormal weather conditions blew down this wonderful, still healthy tree in May 2007.

• This tree had a girth of 3.8 metres (over 12 feet) and was one of only five known large elms in the Plymouth area.

• There are plans to replace the tree with a species of European elm that is resistant to Dutch elm disease.

• As the wood is tough and free of knots, as well as being close grained and not liable to splitting or cracking, it is very durable under water. It was used for water pipes, before cast iron took over, as well as being used to construct harbours and coffins.

31

WELLINGTONIA
Sequoiadendron giganteum

Location

Overlooking Hooe Lake at Radford Arboretum, this tree can be admired by walking down from the main entrance in Hooe Road, Plymstock.

Story

"Represents the foresight of the Plymstock Civic Society in creating Radford Arboretum – a marvellous amenity for future generations."

Mr Phil Armson

Did you know...

• Soon after it was discovered in the Sierra Nevada region of California in the 1850s, this grand tree was planted on many large estates. The first in England was at Killerton House, Devon, but possibly the most famous was at Stratfield Saye, in Hampshire, the estate of the Duke of Wellington after whom the tree is named.

• It grows well in Britain, although its tall crown is often struck by lightning, killing the top of the tree.

• The thick, spongy bark is fire resistant because it does not contain resin. It is also rich in chemicals and tannins – even after a fallen tree has lain on the forest floor for many years, it does not show much decay.

• Today, were it not for the many National Parks in California, which are protecting this species, there would be few remaining. One called 'General Sherman' has been named as the biggest living thing in the world – 55,040 cubic feet in volume.

DAWYCK BEECH

Fagus sylvatica 'Dawyck'

Location

This splendid tree can be spotted at the top of Royal Parade in the city centre on St. Andrew's Cross roundabout.

Story

"What great design to plant this tree here. Reaching for the sky, its shape complements the church tower of St Andrew as well as the jetting waters of the Gdynia Fountain."

Mr Andrew Young

"It's an unusual tree for the city centre and looks tall and impressive."

Mrs Jackie Perry

Did you know...

• It is called the Dawyck beech because it was discovered growing near Dawyck Gardens in Scotland by the Head Gardener of the estate during the 19th century.

• It is an upright narrow form of the common beech with branches that twist and grow straight upwards. The tree can reach heights of over 25 metres (82 feet).

• It became an instant success with arboriculturists and landscape architects, as it brought the beauty of the beech tree to tight corners of towns and cities.

• Beech trees prefer to grow in the shade and can suffer from sunburn! This is less of a problem for the Dawyck beech as its trunk is surrounded by leaves. With climate change, some people think that beech trees may die out in Southern Europe.

THE COPLESTON OAK
Quercus robur

Location

This tree has an ecclesiastical setting outside St Mary's Church on the corner of Tamerton Foliot Road and Church Row Lane in the village of Tamerton Foliot.

Story

"The tree at Tamerton Foliot is a landmark for the area and Copleston family history. Our heritage needs to be secured for future generations to learn from history and mistakes of the past."

Mr Paul Copleston

"I nominate the oak tree by St. Mary's Church Tamerton Foliot, where I lived as a child. It always seemed so mysterious to us, how it continued to grow despite its completely hollow trunk."

Mrs Christine Mudge

Did you know...

• The tree is named after Christopher Copleston, a wealthy local landowner who killed his godson in 1562, reputedly with a dagger, under its branches. By surrendering some of his estates, Copleston was pardoned from the gallows by Queen Elizabeth I and two years later he became a Justice of the Peace! A tablet under the tree commemorates the name.

• The Copleston Oak is one of only 750 oaks in Britain that have nationally recognised names.

• It was fortunate not to have been cut down for shipbuilding, probably because it was a famous local landmark.

37

INDIAN BEAN TREE

Catalpa bignonioides

Location

This exotic tree can be found just by the entrance to Central Park on the corner of Inverdene and Barn Park Road.

Story

"This Indian bean tree is over 70 years old and has a beautifully symmetrical spherical shape. In the summer the huge pale green leaves stand out against the trees behind it and provide a gentle shade and refuge from the heat of a sunny day. In winter the pinky grey trunk and the long beans dangling from even the thinnest branches make it a splendid sight."

Mr Graham Lang

Did you know...

• It was discovered in Virginia, USA and brought to Britain in 1726 when Plymouth was a major transatlantic port.

• Its name derives from an American tribe of Indians, the Catawba, who lived in the area where the tree was found.

• This is the last tree species to come into leaf, sometimes as late as June.

• Its huge leaves collect and filter dust and pollution, significantly improving air quality in cities.

• The tree produces large white, candle shaped flowers in July and August, which give rise to long, slender bean pods.

• Some fine veterans are planted near the Houses of Parliament in London.

BLACK WALNUT

Juglans nigra

Location

This beautiful tree, on National Trust land, can be viewed from the Orange Grove in the gardens of Saltram House. The entrance is via the Visitor Reception.

Story

"My brother, John Hannaford, loved walnut trees and catalogued all the walnut trees he came across on his walks. After John died we planted a walnut tree in his memory. We sent all the walnut tree locations to the Walnut Society, and now we walk where he would have walked and look at the trees he found. This lovely tree at Saltram was special to him."

Mrs P.L. Hannaford-Janes

Did you know...

• The timber of the walnut tree is highly prized for furniture, and was used for gun stocks, as the wood is able to absorb the shock of recoil, it does not splinter and is smooth to the touch.

• During the 18th and 19th centuries the phrase 'to shoulder walnut' meant to enlist as a soldier.

• In the 18th century hard winters caused a shortage of home grown walnut so cabinet makers were forced to use black walnut imported from the New World, where it grew in abundance.

• John Tradescant, gardener to King Charles I recorded that he had a black walnut tree in his London garden in 1633. He visited Plymouth and persuaded ships' captains to bring back the seeds from North America.

SILVER PENDENT LIME

Tilia x petiolaris

Location

These trees can be found in Plympton. Take the footpath off Dark Street Lane, which leads to the Health Centre. The two limes are there.

Story

"Off Dark Street Lane there are a lot of mature trees, formerly in the grounds of 'Sydney' built in 1800 and demolished in 1955, when Colonel Arthur Mudge died. In early summer the leaves are a beautiful light green and later on when in flower, the fragrance of these trees makes it a joy to walk this path, even if the end point is a visit to the doctor. The trees form a green canopy over the path and in the autumn the ground transforms into a golden carpet of fallen leaves. It is splendid to behold."

Mrs Christine Mudge

Did you know...

• The pendent lime is so called because its leaves have a long leaf stalk, which causes the foliage to droop. With its downward sweeping branches it is sometimes known as the weeping white lime.

• The leaves are white underneath and appear silvery when bathed in sunlight.

• The pendent lime is always grafted and the graft line on this tree can be clearly seen at 2 metres (6 feet) up the trunk.

• The nectar from the highly fragrant flowers is a narcotic to bumble bees. They can be seen flying drunkenly under the boughs of the tree.

COPPER BEECH

Fagus sylvatica f. *purpurea*

Location

This tree stands in the private grounds of Pocklington Rise, which provides housing for the visually impaired. As such it is necessary to gain permission to see the tree by telephoning 01752 339553. Pocklington Rise is at the top of George Lane near Ridgeway.

Story

"The tree is very beautiful in full leaf or without and has an unusual feature where a branch has come off the main branch and grafted to the side of another offshoot. The girth is huge."

Mrs Debbie Waller

"I find the shape of the branches twisting skywards and linking to each other fascinating. It could even be a sculpture."

Mr D Price

Did you know...

• Beech often produces contorted and crossing branches that graft themselves onto other branches or stems. The Pocklington Rise tree has a grafted branch between its two main stems giving it an unusual feature and greater strength as well.

• This copper beech has slightly different colours from the one at Ford Hill. This is caused by different amounts of xanthocyanin pigment in the leaves.

• The bark of most tree species becomes rougher and more divided as the tree gets older. Beech can easily be recognised by its smooth, silvery-grey bark that does not change with age.

SWEET CHESTNUT
Castanea sativa

Location

This tree can be discovered at the rear of a block of garages in Pode Drive, opposite Bellingham Crescent in Plympton.

Story

"This tree is probably the largest sweet chestnut outside of Saltram. It has survived development as new 'layers' of landscape have been added around it. The tree is probably a few hundred years old."

Mr C Knapman

"We love the way the tree curves into the hillside following the lay of the land."

Local Residents

Did you know...

• The tree was introduced to Britain by the Romans, who ate a kind of porridge made from its nuts ground up with milk. This porridge or "pollenta" as it is also known is still popular in southern Europe today.

• Today we have the tree to thank for roasted chestnuts and chestnut stuffing at Christmas, although most of the chestnuts used for these delicacies are not British, as our climate is not warm enough to produce the full sized nuts required.

• Few sweet chestnut trees are wild as they do not germinate freely here. Most have been planted in parks and gardens.

• Chestnut trees are long lived and develop a distinctive spiral pattern on the bark as they grow older. These patterns are great for tree rubbings.

THE GATEWAY BEECH
Fagus sylvatica

Location

Situated on the central reservation of the A386 just after the Woolwell roundabout when leaving Plymouth to go towards the Moor, this tree is best seen from the footbridge nearby.

Story

"An amazing tree standing amongst the urban sprawl. Fantastic shape and lovely to look at when sat in traffic jams."

Ms Mel Holt

"This must have grown in a farm hedge once upon a time and now it is on the central reservation of a dual carriageway."

Mr James Roberts

Did you know...

• The low form and sheared crown shape of the tree have probably resulted from its exposure to strong winds in this location.

• The nuts, known as mast, are edible but too many may cause headaches because of their high levels of potash.

• In former times beech mast was used to feed pigs.

• Beech supports up to 100 different insects, some of which live off the foliage and others in the deadwood of older hollow trees.

IRISH YEW

Taxus baccata 'Fastigiata'

Location

A magnificent setting in the churchyard of St. Budeaux Church, found on The Green at Higher St. Budeaux, by the roundabout to the Tamar Bridge.

Story

"Sir Francis Drake married Mary Newman here in 1569 – a church steeped in history. I reckon the church and its churchyard is one of the best in the country and the fine yew trees add to its charm – they are so well tended and in excellent condition."

Mrs Jackie Knapman

Did you know...

• The Irish yew is so called because it was first discovered growing in the Cuilcagh Mountains, County Fermanagh, Ireland, around 1770. It was propagated by cuttings with each tree directly related to the original one.

• It has curved needles and a more upright growth habit than the common yew. One of the garden forms has yellow needles. The Irish yew is an excellent choice of tree for ornamental hedging.

• The poisonous fruit – a single seed – is held in a fleshy red casing called an aril which has an opening at the top to help the seed to ripen.

• In the early 19th century Irish yew became popular as an architectural plant, whereas its parent, the common yew, has long been favoured to create imaginative topiaries in the gardens of stately homes.

JUDAS TREE

Cercis siliquastrum

Location

This tree is growing in the front garden of number 18 Thorn Park, a private house in a Victorian square in Mannamead.

Story

"In spring this tree is a mass of pink flowers with hardly a leaf in sight."

Mr Chris Hunt

"We liked this tree so much that we planted a young one in the grounds of Thorn Park. It is such a delight. We try to plant more unusual trees – this one certainly fits the bill."

Mannamead Conservation Society

Did you know...

• The tree was introduced before 1600 from the eastern Mediterranean area, and may have got its name from Judaea, the area of Israel where the tree is quite common.

• Another story is that the tree is named after Judas Iscariot who hanged himself on this tree after betraying Jesus, explaining the tree's naturally crooked stems.

• The tree prefers a mild, sunny climate which is why it does so well in this area.

• The tree is a member of the pea family. The pink, pea-like flowers open in late spring, growing directly from the branches and the trunk, before the leaves emerge.

• The flowers, sometimes two centimetres long, change into pinkish pods during autumn.

53

LIME AVENUE

Tilia x europaea

Location

Making a wonderful statement these trees can be found in Devonport Park along the path that runs south through the park from Exmouth Road just along from the tennis courts.

Story

"The avenue of limes is beautiful in all seasons; summer time with their heavy laden branches creating a tunnel of dappled shade; autumn, dressed in their glorious autumnal colours and winter with their bare branches giving shelter from the wind and the rain; but my favourite time is in the month of May when their dainty, pale green leaves make their appearance. Long may they stand proud".

Mrs Angela Turner

Did you know...

• This avenue was planted shortly after Devonport Park was created in 1858 and provides a magnificent feature.

• The common lime is a hybrid of the large-leaved lime and the small-leaved lime. In the 18th century, many were imported from Holland to be planted in the gardens of stately homes.

• Tolerant of poor conditions it softens harsh urban landscapes when planted as a street tree.

• The timber is valued for intricate wood carving and is also used to make musical instruments such as the harp and piano soundboards.

• Morris Men choose lime for their sticks because when they 'thwack' their partner's sticks the wood does not splinter.

LUCOMBE OAK

Quercus x *hispanica* 'Lucombeana'

Location

From the entrance to Widey Wood, by Widey Lane in Crownhill, walk about 50 metres south, off the main footpath in order to find this tree.

Story

"This must be the biggest tree in Plymouth. I come here every day to walk the dog – the splendour of this tree never ceases to amaze me."

Local Resident

Did you know...

• Mr Lucombe was an Exeter nurseryman in the eighteenth century. He propagated thousands of these trees which are a cross, or hybrid, between the cork oak and the Turkey oak.

• The tree in Widey Wood has a girth of 5.5 metres (approximately 18 feet). Hybrid trees, like the Lucombe oak, generally grow quickly and to a large size.

• Mr Lucombe was reported to have had his original tree sawn up, the planks being stored under his bed to provide wood for his coffin. They were there a long time as he lived to the grand old age of 102.

• There are no commercial uses for Lucombe oak timber.

• The two native oaks – English and sessile – were always used for naval shipbuilding.

PLYMOUTH PEAR

Pyrus cordata

Location

Make your way to lower E car park at Derriford Hospital, walk along Morlaix Drive toward the ambulance depot. It is the first tree on the right after the car park.

Story

"I became aware of the existence of the Plymouth pear in the 1980s when I came across a reference to the original discovery of the tree in 1865."

"I realised this was a tree I knew quite well, because in the 1960s I regularly walked the lanes in the area with my family and each autumn scrumped apples growing in a hedge close to a wild pear tree; a pear tree which was totally different from any other I had seen."

"I contacted the Conservation Officer, gave him the notes I had taken and went with him to show him the tree and my assumptions were confirmed."

Mrs Doreen Mole

Did you know...

• Plymouth is one of the few cities to have a tree named after it. It got its name because it was discovered growing near Eggbuckland, in 1865, by the Victorian naturalist Thomas Richard Archer Briggs (1836 - 1891), who lived near Derriford.

• The fruit is hard and small, an ancestor of our modern pear. In the 1990s English Nature included it in their 'Species Recovery Programme' in order to secure its future. Partners included the Royal Botanic Gardens at Kew and Plymouth City Council.

59

OAK
Quercus robur

Location

This dead tree can be seen near the junction of Miller Way and Novorossisk Road at Estover.

Story

"The oak was once a thriving healthy tree of medium/large proportions before the Estover estate was built. In its dead form, it is a constant reminder of our environmental future if we allow this to happen."

Mr Roger Bowden

Did you know...

• In the dictionary, 'estovers' means an entitlement to gather firewood.

• Even when dead, the tree provides interest and a focal point for the local area. It makes a natural sculpture and a place for children to play.

• Dead trees are full of life. They are able to support fungi, lichens, mosses and insects on which birds and animals can feed.

• As old trees decay and break down, nutrients are returned to the soil. These in turn become available for other plants and new growth.

• Dead trees in the landscape are completely natural and should not always be tidied-up. They are part of the circle of life.

MAIDENHAIR TREE

Ginkgo biloba

Location

This particular tree is set within Thorn Park park, Mannamead, in the south east corner.

Story

"In 1986 I retired after forty years as a craftsman gardener with Plymouth Parks. For eighteen years I worked at Thorn Park, in that time I read quite a lot about the ginkgo biloba tree and the versatile herb which has been taken from the tree and has eased the suffering for many people, so it will be my favourite tree."

Mr Stan Hunt

Did you know...

• Fossils of the maidenhair tree have been found in coal seams formed 250 million years ago. This ancient tree is the only survivor of its family, being neither conifer nor broadleaf.

• Unlike other trees which rely on wind or living things to carry their pollen, the maidenhair tree has free swimming male sperm which move along rain-drenched branches to reach the ovules.

• The unusual shaped leaves, partly divided in the middle, give rise to the tree's common name as they resemble those of the maidenhair fern.

• Under the instigation of the Mannamead Conservation Society and the Park Pharmacy Trust in the 1980s, the maidenhair tree was planted as a street tree around Thorn Park, one of the few remaining Victorian squares in Plymouth.

HORSE CHESTNUT

Aesculus hippocastanum

Location

Set in the beautiful Beaumont Park, in St Jude's, off Tothill Avenue, these trees can be found in the centre of the park.

Story

"As a child I spent endless hours in the park and much of it under these trees. In autumn we would be on the hunt for conkers and I can still feel the excitement we felt shuffling through the fallen leaves looking for the gleaming brown treasures. My friends and I would arrive as early as possible and spend every second there before school and again after school and much of Saturday too. I probably spent more time in the company of these trees than with my family. Regretfully we rewarded the trees by hurling at the branches anything we could find to dislodge the conkers. I'm sure we did more damage than we either imagined or desired but the trees proved very hardy. I still visit the trees and it seldom requires more than a few minutes before I am transported back to the 1960s. So much has changed but the trees remain a towering constant. I hope the occasional hug I give them now makes up for my taking them for granted all those years ago."

Mr M J Rogers

Did you know...

• Beaumont Park formed the walled grounds of Beaumont House. In 1892, the Borough of Plymouth bought the house and grounds for £26,000. Beaumont Park was opened as the town's first recreation ground, after The Hoe.

• Over three hundred trees grow in the park today and they create an oasis of calm near the city centre.

BOUNDARY OAKS
Quercus robur

Location

After parking the car at Saltram House, take the path towards the river estuary. At the cow crush, take the tarmac path until you reach a five bar gate. The grand oaks are in this field.

Story

"I believe they are important, as they stand as unique historical waymarkers. We stand by their sides in the 21st century, with all our advances of technology, but they are timeless. They have simply grown and grown, sometimes more, sometimes less, but have remained a constant feature throughout our recorded history"

Mr John Banfield

Did you know...

• The Boundary Oaks are estimated to be over 500 years old and were there before the Parker family started to build Saltram House in the 1740s. The trees would have originally marked the boundary between different estates.

• John Smeaton, who was chosen to build the third Eddystone Lighthouse, copied the shape of oak trunks for its design. Some critics doubted whether it could withstand the force of the waves, but the lighthouse lasted for 123 years until 1882 and was only then taken down because the rock on which it stood was being undermined by the sea.

• Interestingly, the jay is responsible for planting the majority of oak trees as they collect and bury the acorns for winter feeding. They do not find them all leaving some to grow as seedlings.

BEECH
Fagus sylvatica

Location

This tree stands at the front of Charlton Residential Home, on the corner of Mannamead Road and Mutley Road.

Story

"Massive example of a mature beech, very imposing and prominent and the root base is fantastic."

Mr Chris Hunt

"In spring time, its pale leaves edged with silvery hairs bring a fresh look to this corner. Sometimes I can see imaginary creatures and faces in the buttressed roots. The delicate tracery of the branches in winter must be one of the most beautiful sights in the city."

Anonymous

Did you know...

• This tree is probably about 120 years old and may have been planted by the first residents of Charlton House. They would be surprised to see how large it has grown.

• The shape of this tree with its full-domed crown is quite different from the Gateway Beech because of the different growing influences such as wind and sun.

• Anglo Saxons used thin boards of beech to write on and 'book' derives from the same word as beech.

• Oil has been extracted from the nuts since ancient times. It was used in the preparation of food and sometimes for lighting fires.

SYCAMORE
Acer pseudoplatanus

Location

This clump of trees can be admired at the south-eastern corner of Saltram House (National Trust) car park.

Story

"This group of sycamores represents the last vestige of a very old hedgerow that existed before the park was landscaped in the 18th century. The tree or trees have fused together to form the remarkable and unusual feature we see today. Its natural beauty has given many generations of children a magical place to play and somewhere to feed young imaginations."

Mr John Banfield

Did you know...

• The sycamore tree at Saltram is something of a curiosity as it consists of several stems all connected by a fused mass of buttresses and roots. It may have been caused by management practices in the past such as hedge laying or coppicing.

• Sycamore produces fine grained, white wood which is used to make kitchen utensils like rolling pins and wooden spoons. It is completely odourless and does not taint food.

• It is easy to tell sycamore by its bright red leaf stalks in summer and bright green buds in winter.

• Children play 'helicopters' with sycamore seeds as the wings twirl towards the ground.

LONDON PLANE

Platanus x hispanica

Location

This tree can be found on the campus of the University of Plymouth at North Hill. It is behind the Portland Square building.

Story

"I really like this particular tree because it softens and brings a bit of nature into quite a built up area. The branches reflect wonderfully in the plate glass windows of the Portland Square building behind. It gives a light and airy feeling to the place."

Mrs Jackie Perry

Did you know...

• This tree survived a devastating bomb attack during an air raid in April 1941 which killed 72 people in a nearby air-raid shelter.

• Portland Square was an elegant residential area lined with trees, including this one. The Portland Square building takes its name from it.

• The London plane grows well in cities with severe traffic pollution and it acts as a giant air conditioner and purifier.

• Young trees have beautifully coloured bark mottled with greys and yellows.

• The trunks of older trees are reddish brown or grey-brown with fine vertical fissures and folds.

ST. PANCRAS YEWS

Taxus baccata

Location

Just over the wall in the churchyard at the front of St. Pancras Church, which is in Honicknowle Lane, Pennycross, you will find these yews.

Story

"These two yew trees stand as sentries to the entrance of the churchyard. They have formed fascinating, natural, living sculptures with their contorted trunks and branches."

Mrs Frances Bryant

Did you know...

• The wood from yew trees has been used for making bows (for shooting arrows) since earliest times. Its botanical name, Taxus, comes from 'taxon' which is Greek for bow.

• Most parts of the tree are poisonous and its Greek name gives us 'toxin' and 'toxic'.

• Despite being poisonous, recent research has isolated the anti-cancer drug Taxol from the tree.

• The yew tree is one of Britain's three native conifers; the other two being juniper and Scots pine.

• The oldest yew tree in Britain is estimated to be over 5000 years old – that means it was growing well before Stonehenge was built.

• Yew trees are frequently grown in churchyards. Nobody is quite sure why! It could be a throwback to Celtic times when the tree was revered.

75

BIBLIOGRAPHY

1   Johns, Rev. C.A.; Ed. Cook, E.T.;c.1912.
     British Trees & Shrubs. Routledge: London.
2   Johnson, O. & More, D.; 2004.
     Collins Tree Guide. HarperCollins: London.
3   Lewington, A. & Parker, E.; 1999. Ancient Trees – Trees
     That Live For A Thousand Years. Collins & Brown: London.
4   Mabey, R.; 1996. Flora Britannica.
     Sinclair-Stevenson (Reed International): London.
5   Miles, A.; 1999.
     Silva - The Tree In Britain. Ebury Press: London.
6   Milner, J.E.; 1992. The Tree Book.
     (Channel 4) Collins & Brown: London.
7   Mitchell, A.; 1974. A Field Guide To The Trees Of Britain
     & Northern Europe. Collins: London.
8   More, D. & White, J.; 2003. Cassel's Trees Of Britain &
     Northern Europe. Cassel (Weidenfeld & Nicholson): London.
9   Pakenham, T.; 1996. Meetings With Remarkable Trees.
     Weidenfeld & Nicholson: London.
10 Pakenham, T.;2002. Remarkable Trees Of The World.
     Weidenfeld & Nicholson: London.
11 Paterson, J.M.; 1996. Tree Wisdom. HarperCollins: London.
12 Rodger, D., Stokes, J. & Ogilvie, J.; 2003. Heritage Trees
     of Scotland. Tree Council: London.
13 Stokes, J. & Rodger, D.; 2004. The Heritage Trees Of
     Britain & Northern Ireland. (Tree Council) Constable: London.
14 Tudge, C.; 2005. The Secret Life Of Trees – How They Live
     & Why They Matter. Penguin: London.
15 Miles, A.; 2006. The Trees that made Britain.
     BBC Books: London.
16 Harris, E & J; 1981. Field Guide to the Trees and Shrubs
     of Britain. The Reader's Digest Association Ltd: London.
17 Addison, J.; 1999. Treasury of Tree Lore.
     Andre Deutsch Ltd: London.